APACHE HELICOPTERS

BY DENNY VON FINN

EPIC

BELLWETHER MEDIA • MINNEAPOLIS, MN

EPIC BOOKS are no ordinary books. They burst with intense action, high-speed heroics, and shadows of the unknown. Are you ready for an Epic adventure?

This edition first published in 2013 by Bellwether Media, Inc.

No part of this publication may be reproduced in whole or in part without written permission of the publisher. For information regarding permission, write to Bellwether Media, Inc., Attention: Permissions Department, 5357 Penn Avenue South, Minneapolis, MN 55419.

Library of Congress Cataloging-in-Publication Data

Von Finn, Denny
 Apache helicopters / by Denny Von Finn.
    p. cm. – (Epic books: military vehicles)
 Includes bibliographical references and index.
 Summary: "Engaging images accompany information about Apache helicopters. The combination of high-interest subject matter and light text is intended for students in grades 2 through 7"–Provided by publisher.
 ISBN 978-1-60014-816-3 (hbk. : alk. paper)
 1. Apache (Attack helicopter)–Juvenile literature. I. Title.
 UG1232.A88V66 2013
 623.74'63–dc23   2012002393

Printed in the United States of America, North Mankato, MN.

TABLE OF CONTENTS

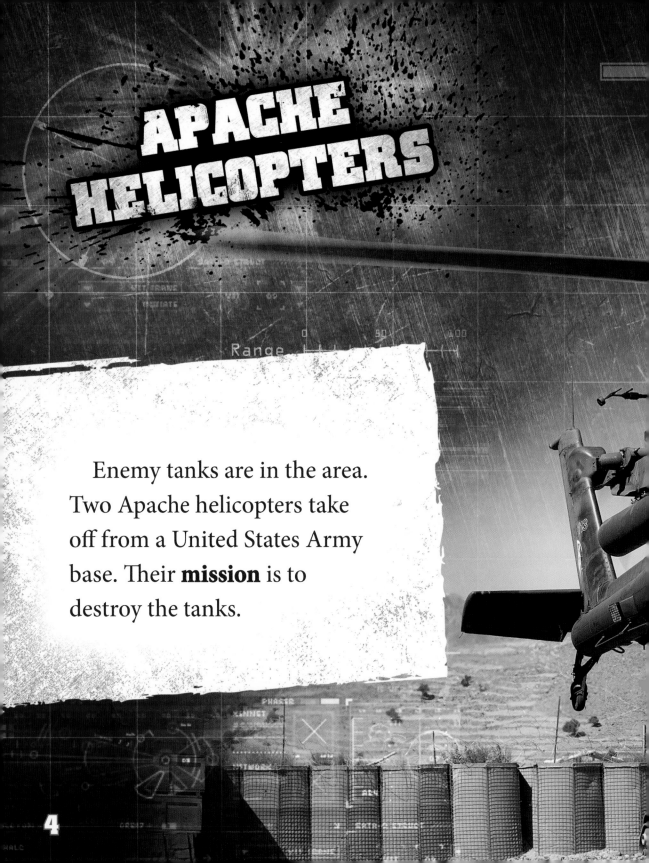

APACHE HELICOPTERS

Enemy tanks are in the area. Two Apache helicopters take off from a United States Army base. Their **mission** is to destroy the tanks.

THREAT DETECT

High-tech cameras on the Apaches sense heat from the tank motors. The pilots race toward the enemy. They ready their weapons.

Missiles fly through the sky. The tanks explode. The Apaches return to base. Their mission was a success!

Apache Fact

The name *Apache* comes from a Native American tribe. The tribe was famous for its skilled warriors.

CREW, PARTS, AND WEAPONS

CO-PILOT GUNNER

Two crew members control the Apache. The pilot flies the helicopter. The **co-pilot gunner (CPG)** finds targets.

PILOT

Apache Fact

The Apache has thick armor to protect the crew. It is sometimes called a "flying tank."

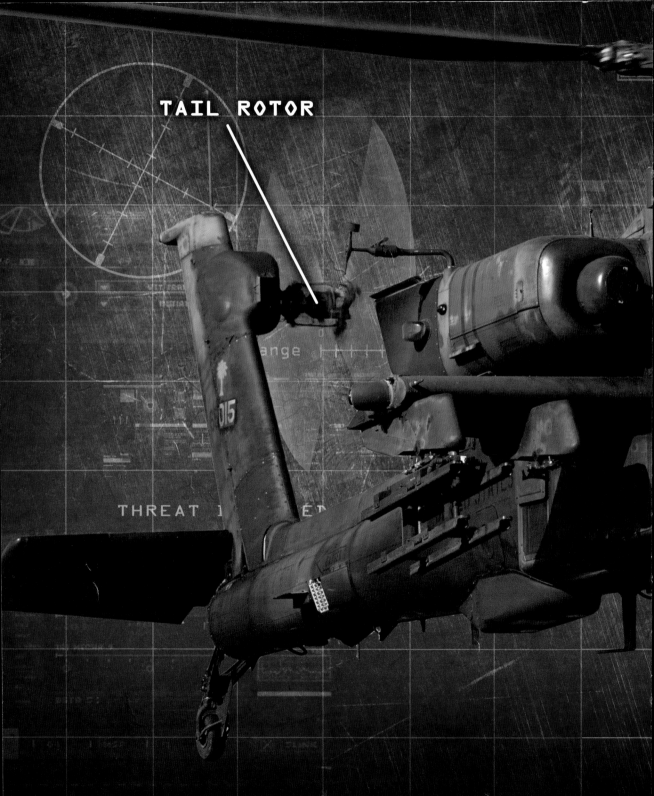

TAIL ROTOR

TOP ROTOR

The Apache has two **rotors**. The top rotor gives the Apache **lift**. The tail rotor helps steer the helicopter.

The Apache uses missiles, **rockets**, and a 30mm **machine gun**. The gun carries 1,200 **rounds**. It is linked to the CPG's helmet. The CPG looks at the target to aim the gun.

THREAT DETECTED

Apache Fact

An Apache machine gun can fire 625 rounds per minute!

APACHE MISSIONS

Apaches are mainly used to destroy enemy vehicles. They also **escort** other aircraft and give **air support** to ground units.

Apaches are most deadly at night. **Night vision** helps crews see in the dark. **Radar** can find more than 250 targets at once.

NIGHT VISION

VEHICLE BREAKDOWN: APACHE HELICOPTER

Used By:	U.S. Army
Entered Service:	1984
Length:	58.2 feet (17.7 meters)
Height:	16.3 feet (5 meters)
Rotor Diameter:	48 feet (14.6 meters)
Weight (Fully Loaded):	16,600 pounds (7,530 kilograms)
Top Speed:	167 miles (269 kilometers) per hour
Range:	300 miles (483 kilometers)
Ceiling:	21,000 feet (6,400 meters)
Crew:	2
Weapons:	30mm machine gun, missiles, rockets
Nickname:	Angel of Death
Primary Missions:	anti-tank attack, air support, escorting

Apaches performed missions in the **Gulf War** and the **War on Terror**. Their firepower makes them deadly on any battlefield.

GLOSSARY

air support—a type of mission that involves flying close to and protecting soldiers on the ground

co-pilot gunner (CPG)—the Apache crew member who controls the weapons and helps fly the helicopter

escort—to travel alongside and protect

Gulf War—a conflict from 1990 to 1991 in which 34 nations fought against Iraq; the war began after Iraq invaded the small country of Kuwait.

lift—the force that allows a helicopter to rise off the ground

machine gun—an automatic weapon that rapidly fires bullets

missiles—flying explosives that are guided to a target

mission—a military task

night vision—a technology that allows pilots and soldiers to see enemies in the dark

radar—a system that uses radio waves to locate targets

rockets—flying explosives that are not guided

rotors—the spinning parts of a helicopter

rounds—ammunition; each round has all of the parts needed to fire one shot.

War on Terror—a conflict that began in 2001; the War on Terror has been fought in Afghanistan, Pakistan, and Iraq.

TO LEARN MORE

At the Library

Bodden, Valerie. *Helicopters*. Mankato, Minn.: Creative Education, 2012.

Peppas, Lynn. *Military Helicopters: Flying into Battle*. New York, N.Y.: Crabtree Pub. Co., 2012.

Von Finn, Denny. *Military Helicopters*. Minneapolis, Minn.: Bellwether Media, 2010.

On the Web

Learning more about Apache helicopters is as easy as 1, 2, 3.

1. Go to www.factsurfer.com.

2. Enter "Apache helicopters" into the search box.

3. Click the "Surf" button and you will see a list of related Web sites.

With factsurfer.com, finding more information is just a click away.

INDEX